The Kingdom of
Tonga
ancient polynesia

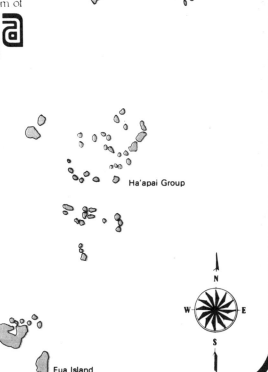

Vava'u Group

Ha'apai Group

N
W E
S

Tongatapu

Eua Island

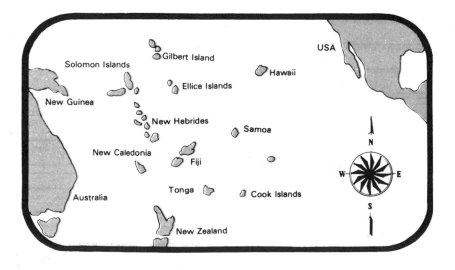

Gilbert Island

Solomon Islands

USA

Hawaii

New Guinea

Ellice Islands

New Hebrides

Samoa

New Caledonia

Fiji

Australia

Tonga

Cook Islands

N
W E
S

New Zealand

TONGA

James Siers

MILLWOOD PRESS

WELLINGTON • NEW ZEALAND

First published 1978, reprinted 1983, 1985, 1987, 1989, 1993.

MILLWOOD PRESS LTD.
291B Tinakori Road
Thorndon
Wellington
New Zealand

Copyright 1978
James Siers

ISBN 0-908582-32-3

Typography and Design by R. J. Henderson

Set by Computype Services Ltd, Wellington, New Zealand.
Printed in Taiwan.

TONGA

The Kingdom of Tonga consists of approximately 150 islands. They begin 15 degrees south of the equator and continue in a line to 23 degrees, 30 minutes south — two minutes south of the tropic of Capricorn. The land area is small. It is only 696 square kilometres. Such statistics, however, say little for the extreme beauty of these islands which glitter from the awsome depth of the blue-black Pacific Ocean, who's immensity threatens to engulf them.

Tonga lies in the heart of Polynesia; the Samoan Islands only just to the north, Niue; the Cook Islands; Tahiti and the islands of French Polynesia to the east and New Zealand to the South. To the west lies the Melanesian archipelago of Fiji. These are its major neighbours. There are others such as Futuna, Wallis (ancient Uvea); Rotuma and the Ellice Islands. And most of these at some stage or other paid tribute to the power of the Tui Tonga — the ancient dynasty of spiritual and temporal kings who ruled Tonga for 1,000 years. Great double canoes were constantly on the move between these islands and even beyond, in quest of new lands.

The Kingdom consists of three principal groups — Tongatapu, which is also the seat of government; Ha'apai, some sixty miles to the north and Vava'u, forty miles to the north-north-east of Ha'apai.

Tonga is the last independent Constitutional Monarchy in Oceania. Its population of 90,000 people is ruled by King Taufa'ahau Tupou IV, the first-born son of Queen Salote, who was not only loved by her people, but endeared herself to the rest of the world with her grace and charm at the coronation of Queen Elizabeth II in London. It was Tonga's big moment. Just as suddenly the Kingdom disappeared again into the remoteness of the Pacific, its people happy that this should be so. In retrospect it seems to have been the wise thing to do. Growing evidence points to Tonga as the founding homeland of the fearless sea rovers we know today as Polynesians. Before the time of Alexander the Great, double canoes carved with stone tools and held together with string made from coconut husk, carried their ancestors from South-east Asia into Papua-New Guinea and then south through the Solomon Islands, the Hebrides and into Fiji. The ancient heritage brought thus to Tonga has been largely retained, whereas in other island archipelagoes, such as Hawaii, it has been irrevocably altered.

The Tongans are descended from people whom scientists have called the "Lapita" people. They have left a distinct trail of pottery fragments from Papua-New Guinea to the Marquesas, more than two thousand miles to the north-east of Tonga.

The pottery fragments are called Lapita after an area in New Caledonia where they were first discovered. The fragments showed a fine, highly decorated ware, usually found in association with tools and ornaments. As more of these items were found, it became possible to see that they belonged to a distinct culture whose most outstanding feature was an obvious ability to move over large distances of ocean. The voyages seem to have been motivated mainly by trade. So far, most of the sites uncovered have been found on the less fertile and productive coral atolls and reefs in the Solomons and Hebrides, suggesting that the Lapita voyagers were late starters in Pacific settlement, finding the richer volcanic islands already in possession of others. Their capacity to move freely over the open sea, however, meant that they could still obtain the clay for pottery and the obsidian and stone for tools from distant places — sometimes these items are found a thousand miles from their source. The sites uncovered on the main islands and corresponding to the same period, show tools and ornaments made from local material.

While it is relatively easy to move from Indonesia-Philippines to Papua-New Guinea, the Solomons and even to the Hebrides through the Santa Cruz Islands; then on to New Caledonia through the Loyalty Group, the gap between Fiji and the west is nearly 800 miles at the nearest point. It is more than reasonable to believe that the first crossing was made by the Lapita people. Whereas the sites of their occupation in the west are confined largely to the outer islands, in the east in Fiji,

Tonga and Samoa, these sites are widespread, suggesting initial discovery by the race later labelled as the "Vikings of the Sunrise". Meanwhile, those who were left behind appear to have been absorbed by the dark, Negroid Melanesians who in turn benefited by acquiring their voyaging technology, which also led them to Fiji. It is thought that the two groups co-existed in Fiji for a thousand years, before the Lapita people were slowly either absorbed or forced out to the Lau Islands and then Tonga. In Tonga, the finishing touches, both racially and culturally, finally marked the people we now recognise as Polynesian. Carbon dating of early occupation sites show this to have happened before 1200 BC.

The Tongans never abandoned their voyaging. The site uncovered in the Marquesas — north-east of Tahiti, produced pottery fragments of the Lapita type. In 1974 some of these were analysed in New York for their geological content. The analysis showed what many believed: the pottery was made from material found in only one part of the world, the Rewa delta of Fiji and therefore, the movement had been west to east. The same type of fragments found in Tonga, also showed their Fijian origin. The Tongans, therefore not only maintained links with Fiji, but quested for new lands, continuing this custom into the post-European era. In fact, had it not been for European intervention, the Tongans would have won back most of eastern Fiji, while continuing to exact tribute from other island groups.

Much of Tonga's political power stemmed from a strong central Government, ruled by the Tui Tonga, a line of sacred kings whose dynasty survived for a thousand years. In the thirteenth century, the Tui Tonga appointed his younger brother as his executive. The title was the Tui Haa Takalaua. At a later stage again, the Tui Takalaua appointed one of his sons to a newly created office as the Tui Kanokupolu. In time, the office of the Tui Tonga became comparable to that of a constitutional monarch — he had the title, but the power was held by someone else; almost classically Japanese. The Shogun (military overlord) virtually holding the sacred Emperor captive. Eventually the Tui Kanokupolu line absorbed the Tui Haa Takalaua and then, in the turbulent post-European period, extinguished that of the Tui Tonga.

The man who did this was outstanding for his time — Taufa'ahau Tupou, the self-styled King George the First. He did this by conquest. The present king is the fourth of the line.

King Taufa'ahau Tupou I accepted Christianity, emancipated serfs and Westernised the administration of his Kingdom while retaining ancient Polynesian customs and rituals.

Tonga was discovered by Europeans more than one hundred years before the discovery of Tahiti and some of the other island archipelagoes in the Pacific. The first visitors were the Dutch. They came on two occasions. The first were Schouten and Lemaire who found Niuatoputapu and Niuafoou in 1616. They also observed large Tongan double canoes on the open sea. One of these carried on board two smaller outrigger canoes. In 1643 Abel Tasman discovered southern Tonga, calling at 'Eua, Tongatapu and Nomuka. He found the natives peaceful, orderly and industrious. In 1767 the discoverer of Tahiti, Samuel Wallis, was the next to touch Tonga. After him came Captain James Cook, also an Englishman, but now acknowledged as one of the most outstanding sailors of all time. Unaware that the Tongans were planning to kill him and his crew and seize the ship, he named the group the Friendly Islands.

Not so lucky were the sailors of the British privateer, the *Port Au Prince*, whose ship was seized by Finau Ulukalala at Lifuka Island in Ha'apai. Most of them were massacred. Those who were spared, including Will Mariner, were obliged to join him in the wars of that period. Mariner's account of his life with the Tongans is now regarded as a classic. Those who read it today realise that life has changed little in matters of custom and attitude since Mariner's time. The destruction of the *Port Au Prince* has given Tonga its own treasure legend. Unaware of the value of gold, the Tongans left most of the gold coin untouched. Though some official and unofficial attempts have been made to recover the treasure, it is believed that most of it is still resting on the bottom of the sea.

The present-day discoverer of Tonga will find much to charm him. From the moment the compact, sleek Air Pacific BAC 1-11 jet begins its descent to Fua'amotu Airport, sweeping in over the small islands from the north, from Fiji, or over the rugged southern coast from New Zealand, the visitor feels a quickening sense of adventure; this is Cook's Tonga, Mariner's Tonga, Tonga of ancient kings and demi-gods; beautiful islands, peaceful and quiet, undisturbed, unspoiled, uncommercialised.

The jet lands at Tongatapu and the visitor disembarks to go through immigration and customs formalities in a friendly atmosphere which sets the tone for the visit. Next comes an unhurried drive into town to a choice of accommodation. The Dateline Hotel offers first class tourist accommodation but there are a number of motels and guest houses which are typically Tongan: ultra friendly and concerned for their guest's welfare. As the majority of these are located in Nukualofa, it is possible to visit places of interest on foot. There is the Palace and Chapel on the waterfront; the Royal Tombs nearby; the markets, where the stall-holders proudly display the abundant produce of Tonga's rich soil — tomato, cucumber, cabbage, lettuce, peppers, melons, citrus fruits in season, papaya and mango and the taro and yam for which Tonga is famous. There are many other things besides, including souvenirs. The people are justly famous for their handicrafts, specially tapa cloth made from the bark of a tree and beautiful basketware. Nukualofa bursts into colourful life when visiting cruise ships call. From the Queen Salote Wharf vendors set up open stalls along Vuna Road to the Fa'onelua Gardens where the peak of activity occurs. Near the Palace by the Vuna Wharf there is a daily fish market, the catch sold almost as quickly as it comes ashore. There are octopus, clams, shellfish of all kinds, as well as tropical reef fish and the bigger fish of the open sea. Periodically, most of Nukualofa turns out to purchase whale meat caught by the Cook family. Saturday echoes to the vigour of Tongans at sport and in direct contrast, the next day reigns serenely peaceful. It is an offence under law to break the Sabbath and the visitor finds much to his surprise that the law even applies to taxi drivers. It is a day for church and rest.

There are a number of points of interest in the countryside. The most amazing is the sight at Kolovai where thousands of flying foxes, deemed sacred, hang head downward from a grove of causerina trees all day.

The high-pitched noise carries over a large area and so too does the smell. Across from Kolovai on the western shore, great breakers boom against the reef, sending waterspouts as high as thirty metres into the air. The visitor will find easy transportation to Houma where most sightseers are taken to view the spectacle. To the east, the greatest spectacle is to be found at Lapaha, the ancient capital. Two huge terraces, faced off with coral slabs, hold the remains of generations of the Tui Tonga line. It is said that the coral slabs were cut in Uvea (modern-day Wallis Island) some 800 miles to the north-west and fetched down in great double canoes. As each slab weighs several tonnes, the project must have required the work of many men. The Ha'amonga trilithon, known as the Ha'amonga-A-Maui (the burden of Maui) faces the east between the villages of Afa and Niutoua. The function of this archway was not known. The fact that it was ascribed to the Polynesian hero and demi-god Maui, who seemed to roam the seas raising new lands, may have presented a clue. Tradition states that the trilithon was built about AD 1200 by the eleventh Tui Tonga. It was not until 1967, the year of the coronation of King Taufa'ahau Tupou IV that its function was determined. His Majesty suspected that the Ha'amonga must have served a specific purpose. On 21 June 1967, the King was present at the trilithon at dawn and was rewarded when the sun rose at the exact point indicated by his interpretation of the lines etched on the lintel stone. The information thus obtained would have been invaluable to both navigators and planters in determining the seasons.

'Eua Island is only five minutes by air or, more than two hours by ferry. In contrast to the flat terrain on Tongatapu 'Eua is hilly, with a good stand of native bush. The island is an ideal retreat for hikers, naturalists and ornithologists. It also has an outstanding scenic feature — the precipice on the eastern shore. The cliff falls away nearly 350 metres to the sea below where great combers smash against it, sending waterspouts up its face — incredibly nearly to the top (see picture). There is motel accommodation and transport can be arranged. The visitor should go to some effort to make sure of such arrangements.

There are several attractive beaches both on 'Eua and Tongatapu, but the most outstanding are to be found in the "motu" (islands) which dot the sea in front of Nukualofa. Among these is Pangai Motu. This is owned by The Royal Family, but has been made available to visitors who can make arrangements at an office near the Dateline Hotel. Among the more unusual attractions is the chance to sail a gaff-rigged Tongan whaling boat. The grandfather of Thomas and Albert Cook came from New Zealand about the middle of the last century. He would sail his boat in search of whales, hand-harpooning them and bringing them back to the waterfront where the meat would be cut and sold. His son took up the same occupation and was active until 1975 when he died after a vigorous whale chase, having harpooned, secured and killed the whale, he fell dead in his boat. Arrangements can be made with Tom Cook (when he is not whaling) for a day's cruise to one of the motu where his family will prepare a Tongan picnic lunch while the visitor swims in crystal-clear water off a snow-white beach.

Most visitors are content with Tongatapu, unaware of the extreme beauty of the Ha'apai and Vava'u groups. There is a daily air link operated by South Pacific Island Airways and Tonga Air and well worth the price. The Ha'apai Islands feature outstanding beaches, coupled with peace and tranquility. The administrative centre is on the island of Lifuka where the airstrip is sited. A most exciting strip. You sweep in over the reef where the *Port Au Prince* was taken and burned. The aircraft rushes forward onto the coral runway. Just as you think it will plunge into the ocean beyond, it pulls up smartly and then taxis back to the little terminal. It is easy enough to hire a punt with an outboard, or even a cutter to go exploring the nearby islands and, should you chose, even the volcanic cone of Kao Island, next to Tofua, where an active volcano still smoulders. A feature of the Ha'apai group is the extreme clarity of water and the profusion of coral reefs and fishes.

It was at Lifuka that Captain Cook anchored, naming the Tongan chain the Friendly Islands.

Like James Cook, the visitor can also go to Ha'apai by sea. The voyage from Nukualofa usually takes about eight hours. It takes about the same amount of time to travel by sea to Vava'u — obviously, only a fraction of that time by air. In direct contrast to the flat coral islands of the Ha'apai group, Vava'u is hilly. The approach by sea is outstandingly spectacular. There is a maze of outer islands, each fringed by dazzling white coral beaches or sheer cliffs. Next the vessel passes the narrows between the island of 'Utungake and the distinct massive of Tu'anuku, before entering the tranquil waters of the Port of Refuge. A fleet could safely ride out the most devastating tempests here. The favoured anchorage for visiting yatchsmen is just below the Port of Refuge Hotel, a kilometre past the township of Neiafu.

Among the outstanding places of interest is Mariner's Cave on the island of N'uapapa, about an hour's run by boat from Neiafu. The cave can only be entered by those who can swim underwater. Having arrived at the spot the visitor must summon courage, dive down some two metres and then swim another two or three metres under an overhang before emerging into the eerie light of the cave. I got there with a boatman who refused to dive with me. The prospect was daunting. From the outside going in, only darkness greets the diver. By looking up, it is possible to see where the rock overhang has finished. Then a cautious ascent is made — not too fast in case you emerge to bang your head on rock. The legend of the cave is beautiful. A young chief many years ago discovered it while diving for fish. He was in love with a beautiful girl whose family had been condemned to death for rebellion against the ruling despot. He got her away before she was taken to be put to death and hid her in the cave, visiting her when he could with food and fresh water. In the meantime he prepared a voyaging canoe for a trip to Fiji. On the day of departure his family and friends urged him to take a wife, remarking that he would be lonely otherwise. He replied that the sea would provide. The canoe was anchored near the entrance to the cave and the young man disappeared. Just as those on board were becoming concerned for his safety, he emerged with his bride. They lived in Fiji for several years but returned to Vava'us when news reached them of the despot's death.

Will Mariner tells his own story; how he accompanied his patron, Finau Ulukalala into the cave. There, in company with Finau's body-guard he took part in a cave ceremony. I waited in the cave for some time, taking a number of pictures of the entrance and then went out to urge the boatman to follow me. He would not under any circumstances.

So I went back twice again to savour the moment, reflecting that I might never pass this way again. On returning to Neiafu we called at the swallow's cave on the island of Kapa. The entrance was clearly visible as a great chasm in the rock face and there was plenty of room to go inside with the boat. The vaulted roof was covered with swallow nests and below in the limpid water were thousands of sardines.

There are other islands to the north of Vava'u: Niuatoputapu, Tafahi and Niuaf'ou. I never got there, but I wish I had. I need no excuse to go back to Tonga, but should one be necessary, it will be the lure of unexplored islands and coral reefs.

Acknowledgements

It is obvious that my Tongan assignment would not have been possible without the active help and support of many people. I wish to thank them sincerely — particularly Semisi Taumoepeau and the staff of the Tonga Visitors Bureau; George Wray and South Pacific Island Airways; Tonga Air; Air Pacific and Teta Tours.

During the six weeks I was working in the islands, it was not possible to do everything. For this reason I am specially grateful to Frank Bevacqua who made available his selection of transparencies so that the pictorial coverage of this book would be more comprehensive. Frank first came to Tonga with the Peace Corps but remained in the Kingdom to teach school and continue his interest in photography.

A fascinating glimpse into Tonga's past is offered by the selection of early photographs from the Alexander Turnbull Library. It is remarkable how even relatively recent pictures assume a historical significance.

With this in mind, I hope that those who buy this book will not only enjoy it now for the memories of their visit, but also treasure it for the future when the pictures in it will have become part of Tonga's historical record.   *James Siers*

Queen Salote reviews troops in 1940 when the total population of Tonga was only 32,000 people. In contrast, an old-style warrior poses for the photographer.

The exterior and interior views of the Wesleyan Church at Neiafu in Vava'u, shows the fine workmanship of Tongan craftsmen. Such churches have given way to concrete structures.

An aerial view of Nukualofa, looking west.

Above: HRH the Crown Prince Tupoutoa. *Left:* Fireworks to celebrate the Coronation of King Taufa'ahau Tupou IV in 1967. *Right:* Dancing on the same occasion at Nukualofa.

The Tongans have always been seafarers.

The advent of regular air services has linked Tonga to the outside world. The Air Pacific BAC-111 jet (bottom left), provides a fast service between New Zealand and Fiji, while South Pacific Island Airways maintain a daily schedule between the Tongan island groups.

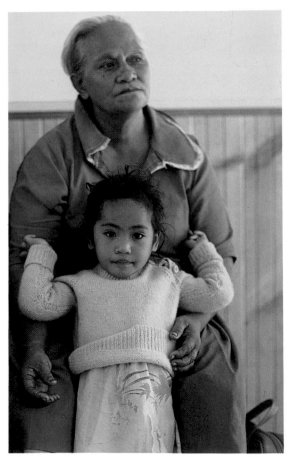

Ancient Tongan customs concerned with births, deaths and marriages, though modified by Christianity, are maintained. Nevertheless, a visitor still gets a shock to see large grave mounds decorated with empty beer bottles and banners.

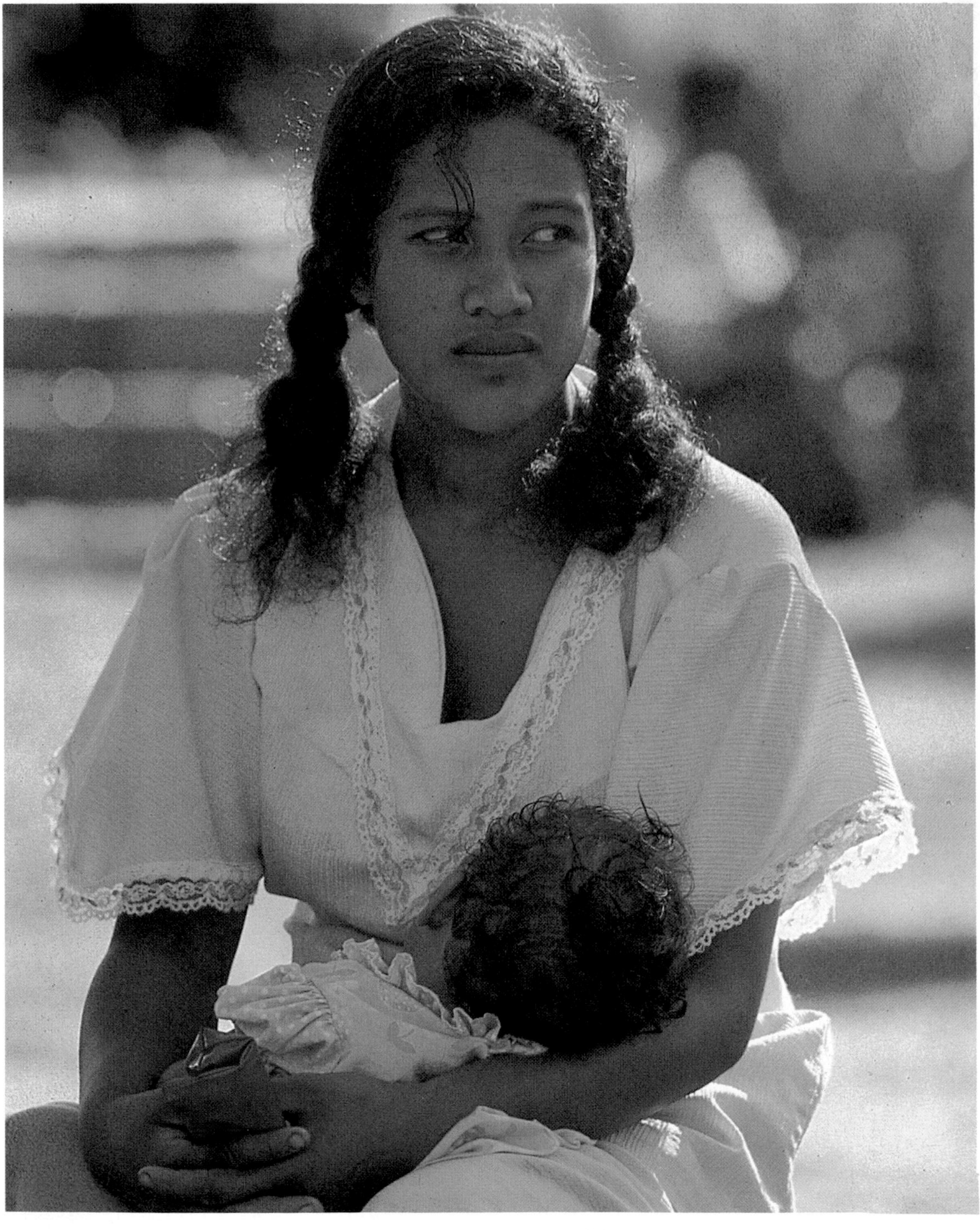

The face of Tonga, found attractive by all who have called there.

Below: The funeral cortège of Queen Salote begins to make its way from the Royal Chapel. The casket, carried by more than one hundred men, is attended by the chief mourners. *Right:* The King and Queen follow the procession to the Royal Tombs.

The Tongans love ritual and ceremonial, whether it is a wedding, such as the one recorded by Frank Bevacqua in Lifuka, or ornate State ceremonial, opposite. *Right:* A visiting German warship receives a 21-gun salute. *Bottom right:* The band marches out from the Royal Tombs enclosure after a wreath-laying

Random camera records the men of Tonga.

Below: His Majesty, King Taufa'ahau Tupou IV, poses at the Palace, Nukualofa. *Top right:* A view of the Palace and Chapel. *Bottom right:* A large tray of food at Pangaimotu on the occasion of a Royal feast.

The crafts of ma
been maintaineᵈ

Left: Tonga's most spectacular island Kao, is captured in these views by Frank Bevacqua. *Above:* The sacred flying foxes of Kolovai.

Above: A young girl climbs a coconut tree, making an attractive picture. *Top right:* The ancient tombs at Lapaha. *Bottom right:* Mature coconuts, split with an axe, form a striking pattern.

Facing page: The hapless leopard shark caught by Albert Cook and, below, the same shark peacefully asleep. *Right:* A yellowfin tuna.

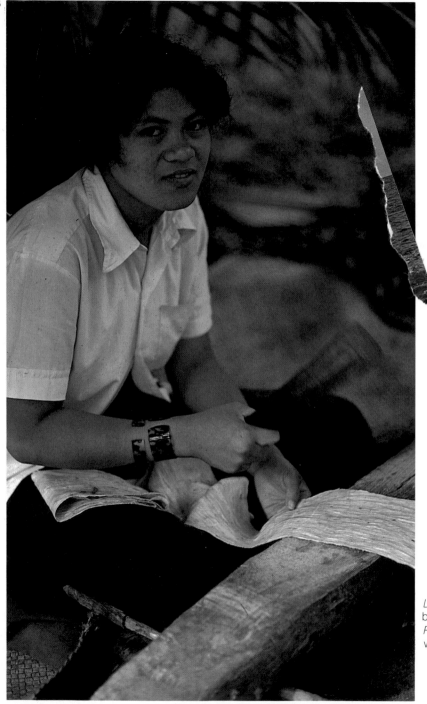

Left: The bark is being beaten out for tapa cloth. *Right:* Tonga's carvers at work.

Tongans are profoundly Christian, lavishing pride in the construction of their churches and religious institutions.

Left: A monument to the Reverend Shirley Baker who played such an important part in the history of the Wesleyan Church in Tonga. Below: The site of Cook's landing at Mu'a, commemorated. Right: The striking reef pattern around one of the islands in Ha'apai.

HERE STOOD FORMERLY THE GREAT BANYAN "MALUMALU - 'O - FULILANG" OR CAPTAIN COOK'S TREE UNDER THE BRANCHES OF WHICH THE CELEBRATED NAVIGATOR CAME ASHORE ON HIS WAY TO VISIT PAU, THE TU'I TONGA (SACRED KING OF TONGA) ON THE OCCASION OF THE INASI (PRESENTATION OF THE FIRST FRUITS) IN THE YEAR 1777.

A random view of Tongan people. *Bottom right:* Thomas Cook, the whaler, sails with his two daughters. The older girl, Eliza, goes whaling as one of the crew.

Left: A vendor offers octopus at Nukualofa. Right: From inside the Swallows Cave, Vava'u, looking out.

Left: A wreath being laid at the Royal Tombs, Nuku-alofa. *Right:* Tonga's defence forces parading near the Palace.

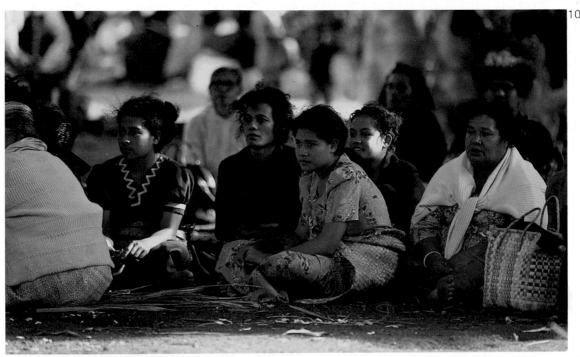

These young dancers are a feature in Nukualofa, performing at the Dateline Hotel and at various functions.

Left: The Ha'amonga-a-Maui, the trilithon at Tonga-tapu. The true nature of the trilithon was discovered by the King in 1967, who found that the trilithon was built by ancient Tongans to determine the seasons.

The photographer has come upon tapa-making,
old-style, with the women of the village joining
together to make the task more social.

An early view of Mount Zion, Nukualofa (just behind and to the side of the Palace). This was once the site of an immense fortress which the Ha'apai chief Finau reduced with the help of canon from the *Port Au Prince.*

In 1947, the King (with glasses) and his brother,
Prince Tuipelehake, were married in a double ceremony in Nukualofa. The occasion, in true Tongan
style, was the cause of great celebration.

The style of the girls with their parasoles and Sunday white, is in marked contrast to the girl posed in the studio.

The ancient tombs at Lapaha, Tongatapu, showing the massive coral slabs which legend says were brought in canoes from Uvea (Wallis Island) some 800 miles to the north-west. The tombs have been cleared of the surrounding vegetation.

This view gives a clue to the style of dress worn in Tonga in pre-Christian times. The men are taking part in playing Lafo.

FOTOFILI
GOV. OF NIUAFOOU

J. AFU

REV. J. B. WATKIN
SUPT. OF VAVAU CIRCUIT

REV. S. BAKER
PREMIER

PRINCE WELLINGTON
GOV. OF VAVAU

An historic photograph, showing some of Tonga's VIPs just before the turn of the century. *Left to right:* The Reverend J. B. Watkin, the superintendent of the Vava'u circuit; Fotofili, the Governor of Niuafoou; J. Afu; the Reverend Shirley Baker, Premier; Prince Wellington, Governor of Vava'u, and Junia, Minister of Finance — so reads the inscription on this early Burton Brothers plate.

The Governor General of New Zealand, Lord Freyberg, meets two Tongan commandos who were attached to American forces in the Solomons in the war against Japan. On the left is Simate Viamake, MM and Silver Cross, and right, Johnny Inukinuha 'Anga, MM and ASC.

The unique mail delivery at Niuafoou was made by passing ships which dropped a sealed can with the mail. It was then taken ashore by canoe. On this account, Niuafoou became known as Tin Can Island.

Ship day is much as it has always been — only the style of clothes change. Even now, canoes sometimes are used, either to go out to the ship, or to bring people back.

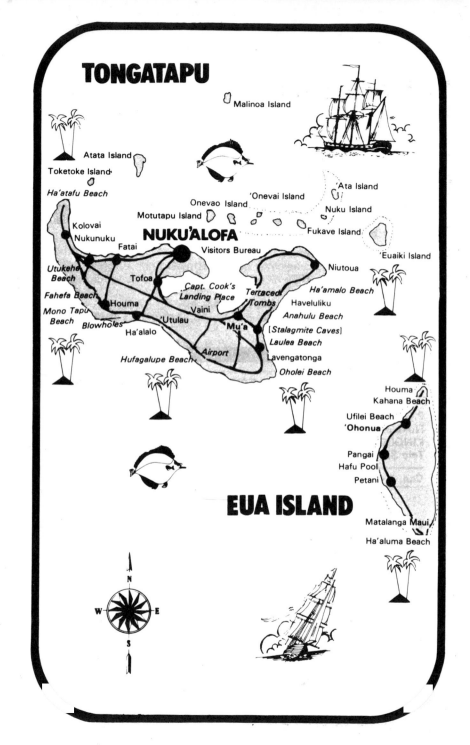

TONGATAPU

Malinoa Island

Atata Island
Toketoke Island
Ha'atafu Beach

'Ata Island
'Onevai Island
Nuku Island
Onevao Island
Motutapu Island
Fukave Island

Kolovai
Nukunuku
Fatai

NUKU'ALOFA

Visitors Bureau

'Euaiki Island

Niutoua

Utukehe Beach
Tofoa
Ha'amalo Beach

Fahefa Beach
Houma
Capt. Cook's Landing Place
Terraced Tombs
Haveluliku

Mono Tapu Beach
Vaini
Anahulu Beach

Blowholes
'Utulau
'Mu'a
[Stalagmite Caves]

Ha'alalo
Laulea Beach

Airport
Lavengatonga

Hufagalupe Beach
Oholei Beach

Houma
Kahana Beach

Ufilei Beach
'Ohonua

Pangai
Hafu Pool
Petani

EUA ISLAND

Matalanga Maui
Ha'aluma Beach

N
W E
S